MW01127524

DAY OF YESHUA

The Simple Guide to Revelation and End Time Prophesy

R. S. HENZERLING

Editor **CLINT WEAVER**

WestBow Press books may be ordered through booksellers or by contacting:

WestBow Press
A Division of Thomas Nelson & Zondervan
1663 Liberty Drive
Bloomington, IN 47403
www.westbowpress.com
844-714-3454

Scripture taken from the King James Version of the Bible.

ISBN: 978-1-6642-0962-6 (sc)
ISBN: 978-1-6642-0964-0 (hc)
ISBN: 978-1-6642-0961-9 (e)

Library of Congress Control Number: 2020920598

Print information available on the last page.

WestBow Press rev. date: 11/10/2020

Welcome to this study of what many consider as the most controversial book of the Bible. Controversial only because many will not touch or talk about it, due to their lack of understanding. This is because of those who "read but do not hear the words" with multiple opinions and speculations about it.

I did not re-invent the wheel here, I believe I just simplified it. This study will be neither opinion or speculation. The cross-referencing of other books of the Bible will be prove that talks about this same great prophecy, to include Jesus' own teaching on the subject, to be fact. My hope is that by the end of this book that you will have a very strong and clear understanding of the book of Revelation and the prophecy of the End Times. "Blessed is he that readeth, and they that hear the words of this prophecy..." Rev. 1:3. I understand that many approach the texts with certain presuppositions, and are reluctant to believe that the Biblical teaching is really that simple to understand, when many have tried before but wouldn't hear what they read. I truly do believe this study will show that it is very simple to understand and that it is plainly explained for us to understand. We just have to want to hear and believe what we read.

CONTENTS

DEDICATION

This book is dedicated to the following:

My late grandparents Lena & Donald Hughes, who always believed in me, took me to church, paid for my youth group activities, and showed me what being Christ like looks like.

My Aunt Naomi and Uncle Eugene for being great Apostolic Christian examples.

My Assistant Pastor, his wife and daughter, Timothy, Priscilla and Abigail Foster for always being there for my family, never judging and always on call to help with life and spiritual issues. You are more than true friends. You are family.

My Pastor and his wife, Kerry and Sheila Sharp for seeing things in me I didn't see and believing in me. For being my shepherds, Christian examples, counselors, leaders and friends. Without you, I would not be where I am in my walk with God.

To my Brother in Christ, Nathan Cotton, for being a great Christ-like friend who helped me understand the Bible, counseled me over coffee at 2 a.m. at IHOP, and taught me how to pray for others and discern spirits.

To my older children, Christopher and Kelsey Henzerling, I wished I had lived a Godly life when I was raising you. I pray every day that you both will find salvation through Jesus Christ.

To my younger children, Ava Knorr, Kale Knorr and Wyatt Henzerling, my Grandson Aiden Artzt and Granddaughter Everleigh Artzt, I aspire to be a Christ-like example of how to live a Godly life through prayer, God's word and worship. I pray that you will have a desire to serve God and worship Him in spirit and in truth. Your salvation is of the utmost importance to me.

To my wife Nickkole Henzerling, you have been my rock in this walk of life. You have picked me up when I was down, taken care of me when I was sick, loved me when I was hard to love, listened to me when I stood in the gap as the spiritual leader of our family and filled the gap when I fell. You have slowed me down when needed, calmed me when I was angered, listened to me when I needed to talk, counseled me when I needed to be counseled, believed in me always, worshipped with me, prayed with me and studied Gods word with me. You have always been by my side. I love you more than yesterday, but not as much as tomorrow.

To my Lord and Savior Jesus Christ, thank you for dying on the cross for my sins, loving me always and for blessing my family abundantly. Thank you, Lord, for using me in ministry and for showing me the biblical truth of your prophecy. Thank you for calling me to write this book. I vow to teach it, live it and stand against false doctrine. "Thanks" seem so inadequate so I will strive to live a life that will lead me to hear the words, "Well done thy good and faithful servant."

INTRODUCTION

The book of Revelation begins with a unique blessing, "Blessed is he that readeth, and they that hear the words of this prophecy, and keep those things which are written therein: for the time is at hand." Rev 1:3. No other book in the Bible begins this way. A blessing according to Revelation 1:3 is given to those who read and hear the words of this prophecy. Hearing is not just hearing the words though, it is also understanding them and responding to them. In the book of Revelation, Jesus uses the words "He that hath an ear, let him hear" 7 times Rev 2:7, 11, 17, 29; 3:6, 12, 22.

It is as if Jesus is stressing the importance as a parent to a child by saying "Pay attention now, this is not an option.". This was also one of Jesus' most common sayings in the Gospels Matt 11:15; 13:9, 43; Mark 4:9, 23; Luke 8:8; 14:35. It is possible to hear and read words, but not recognize, understand or obey what is being said. We are also told to, "…keep those things which are written therein…" Rev 1:3. Jesus is instructing us to understand it. He is urgently communicating to us to take this prophecy seriously, and to allow our knowledge and understanding to affect the way we live our lives.

A grave warning according to Rev. 22:18-19 is given to those who, "...add unto these things...God shall add unto him the plagues that are written in this book...take away from the words of the book of this prophecy...God shall take away his part in the book of life...". No other books of the Bible contain a warning of this severity. Based on the prologue of Revelation first three verses, it is clear that God expects the church to both understand and respond to this prophecy. Understanding doesn't only come by reading and hearing the words, we must keep the things that are written. It is also clear that anyone who adds to or takes away from this prophecy will suffer the consequences for their deceit.

SATAN'S GREATEST DECEIT

Let's start with the understanding that all warfare is based on deception. Hence, when we are able to attack, we must seem unable; when using our forces, we must appear inactive. When we are near, we must make the enemy believe we are far away; when far away we must make the enemy believe we are near. Other terms related to deception are dishonesty; trickery, ruse, sham, fraud, cons, cheating and a whole lot more. If you know your enemy and know yourself, you shouldn't fear the results of a hundred battles. If you do not know either the enemy or yourself, you will succumb in every battle.[i]

Satan is basically utilizing the Sun Tzu concepts upon the world when it comes to the End Times, and he has been doing so for centuries. However, this deceit started around

1830 with a false doctrine. What better way to deceive people and turn them from God, then tell them the lie that they will be "raptured" before the start of Daniels 70th week Dan. 7:15-28, 9:26-27, 11:31, 12:11-13.

Satan understands that if he makes "Christians" believe the lie of a pre-tribulation rapture, and they are not taken away before the introduction of the Son of Perdition Beast and the Great Tribulation persecution of Christians, that they will fall away from God, through deceit of the Beast.

According to II Thess. 2:3, about the coming of the Lord, says, "...that day shall not come, except there come a great falling away first, and that man of sin be revealed, the son of perdition".

The Word rapture rapio Latin- to seize or violently carry off is the equivalent of the greek word a'rpa,zw harpazo meaning to seize or snatch away.

The Latin Vulgate circa 400 Ad uses the word 'rapture' when translating the Apostle Paul's uses of a'rpagnso,meqa harpaghesomatha in I Thess. 4:17, the word is "caught up".

The pre-tribulation rapture doctrine was invented by John Nelson Darby who introduced the doctrine around 1830 AD. All attempts to find evidence on this pre-tribulation doctrine before 1830 has failed with the exception of one individual, Morgan Edwards. Edwards wrote a short essay as a college paper for Bristol Baptist College in 1744 where he confused the second coming with the first resurrection of Rev. 20 and described a pre-tribulation rapture.[ii]

Prior to 1830, no church taught nor believed in their creed, catechism or statement of faith anything about a pre-tribulation rapture. The predominate view regarding the second coming was akin to the pre-tribulation doctrine,[iii] as Matt. 24:29-31 reads "Immediately after the tribulation of those days shall the sun be darkened, and the moon shall not give her light, and the stars shall fall from heaven, and the powers of the heavens shall be shaken: And then shall appear the sign of the Son of man in heaven: and then shall all the tribes of the earth mourn, and they shall see the Son of man coming in the clouds of heaven with power and great glory. And he shall send his angels with a great sound of a trumpet, and they shall gather together his elect from the four winds, from one end of heaven to the other."

After Darby refined the concept, it spread very rapidly throughout Europe and America and was blessed by many within the religious community.[iv] In 1909 a study bible incorporating Darby's invented pre-tribulation doctrine was written by Schofield and is now known as the Schofield Bible.

Darby greatly impacted the religious Christian community, by infecting it with this false doctrine of a "secret reaping". Churches have neither rejected nor approved this doctrine, they simply choose to remain silent about it.

Along those same lines, to openly condemn this false doctrine, thus leaving it open to deceive many of the elect is void in most churches. There are some churches that espouse the exact view as I am expressing within this book; however, many are seeing through a glass darkly and "…prophesy in part…" I Cor. 13.

The precise timing of the second coming of the Lord is not a salvific issue, but I contend that it is an issue that may cause the "…great fallen away…" II Thess. 2:3. If you believe in a pre, mid or post tribulation, it is not assured that you will go to hell; however, it could lead to falling away from your faith or belief. For example, if you believe in a pre-tribulation view, and you are not raptured before the son of perdition shows himself and the Christians face the great tribulation, then you may fall from your belief. It could leave you asking the question, "Why would a God of love allow tribulation to happen to his people?" This is the doubt or the question, that Satan is counting on; individuals who do not heed the teachings the Bible that foretold of a great tribulation.

The Bible clearly tells us to be aware of false prophets and false teachers who will spread and infect false doctrine upon the earth, deceiving man. "And many false prophets shall rise, and shall deceive many." Matt. 24:11

God allowed his people to go through the plagues as outlined in Exod. 8:20-24, 9:4-7, 18, 23-26 and then delivered them. God allowed the prophet to go through the famine, Meshach, Shadrach and Abednego to be thrown into the fire and Daniel to be thrown into the lion's den. Jesus himself was persecuted and killed, so what makes us think that he will deliver us before the tribulation?

I want to explain that God's people are never promised to be immune from tribulation thlipsis, but may be called to give their lives for their faith.

This is shown in these references: Rev. 2:13; 6:9-11; 17:6 and 20:4.[v] Do not confuse the great tribulation for Gods wrath, which comes after the breaking of the 7th Seal.

These days will be shortened approximately 45 days, Dan. 12:11-12, Matt. 24:22 says "...but for the elect's sake those days shall be shortened". Shortened refers to what Daniel talks about in Dan. 12:11-12, "And from the time that the daily sacrifice shall be taken away, and the abomination that maketh desolate set up, there shall be a thousand two hundred and ninety days. Blessed is he that waiteth, and cometh to the thousand three hundred and five and thirty days".

Per the Hebrew calendar, the days were more than twenty-nine and a half days, essentially thirty days. If you take thirty days and multiply them by twelve months, then by seven years, the total is two thousand five hundred and twenty days [30 x 12 x 7=2520]. Half of that is twelve hundred and sixty days, which is three and a half years. From the time the sacrifices stop and the Abomination of Desolation is set up is one thousand two hundred and ninety days 1290. If that is subtracted from the day of the Lords coming catching-up, which is one thousand three hundred and five and thirty days 1335, it is forty-five days. Forty-five days, as told in the Bible, is the approximate time after the Abomination of Desolation to when we are caught-up into the clouds to be with our Lord.

So, who is John Darby, and what were his religious beliefs? John Darby was an Anglo-Irish Bible teacher, an influential figure among the Plymouth Brethren and the founder of the Exclusive Brethren. He is considered to be the father of Dispensationalism and futurism.

John Darby traveled across Britain and Europe widely 1830-1840, giving many lectures to include 11 in Geneva on "The Hope of the Church". This established his reputation as a "interpreter of biblical prophecy". America did not embrace his ecclesiology like it did his eschatology, which is still being propagated in various forms.[vi]

Are we really going to continue to believe a doctrine that was never taught nor believed in until over one thousand and eight hundred years after the Apostle John received and wrote the book of Revelation? Would we be wise to believe a man-made doctrine over the Bible? Of course we shouldn't. For the reasons listed above, I am going to walk us through the prophecy of Revelation from different perspectives in the Bible Isa; Dan.; Joel; Matt. 24; Mark 13; Luke 21; I & II Thess.; II Pet.; Rev. 1-11 and Rev. 12-22, etc.

As we progress through the chronological order of events presented within the prophesy, events will be referenced in at least two locations in the Bible to meet sound doctrine on proper placement of the event.

Chapter	Description of Chapter
1	Introduction
2-3	Letters to the Seven Churches
4-5	Setting the scene in heaven
6	Breaking of the first six seals
12	Birth of Christ and war in heaven
13	Antichrist
7 & 14	144,000 and The Catching Up
15	The last seven plagues and the tabernacle of the testimony
8 & 16:1-9	7th seal 8:1, Trumpets 1-4 8:2-13 and Vials 1-4 16:1-9
9 & 16:10-16	First two woes Trumpets 5-6 & First two woes Vials 5-6
10	Angel & Seven Thunders and the sweet and bitter book
11:1-142	Witnesses, the beast of the bottomless pit
11:15-19 & 16:17	3rd woe Seventh Trumpet & Third woe Seventh Vial
17	Babylon
18	Fall of Babylon
19	Armageddon & 201,000 year reign, Satan's deceit and the Great White Throne Judgment
21-22	New Heaven and New Earth

Note: The book of Revelation is not a book that is entirely in chronological order, in fact the book of Revelation is to be split in half 1-11 and 12-22, as it is written from two different perspectives. The same as Matthew, Mark, Luke and John are written about Jesus' teachings in the gospels. The book of Revelation arranged to be read as shown above.

JESUS'S TEACHING ON THE END TIMES

Jesus»s teaching on the end times Matt. 24, Mark 13 and Luke 21 took place on the Mount of Olives while sitting against the temple wall. Peter, James, John and Andrew listened as Jesus proclaimed the end that is to come. He told of wars and rumors of wars, great buildings collapsing, false prophets and false Christ's teaching bad doctrine, brothers betraying one another and times of affliction.

Jesus warns us often that we should watch for the signs of the end times, so that he not come like a thief in the night. He also asks that we stand ready and not be caught by surprise.

Jesus teaches that "...because iniquity shall abound, the love of many shall wax cold." Matt. 24:12. Iniquity abounding is the immoral and grossly unfair behavior, such as we see today. The behavior includes but is not limited to: abortion, homosexuality, persecution of religious beliefs, the diminishing of the Word of God, and the lack of empathy and feelings.

Jesus specifically tells us that when we see the "abomination of desolation" that is spoken by Daniel, we should take to running and hiding and not go back for anything we left behind. For this is the "great tribulation" that we are to endure. Why would Jesus tell us to watch for the abomination of desolation? Is it because we will be here during this time?

Jesus tells us that during this time of tribulation not to look toward or seek for anyone that others proclaim to be the Messiah. We are also shown the signs that are to happen right before Yeshua returns to take us away. These signs will be explored more in depth as we go through the chapters of this book.

If anyone disagrees with what is written and taught in this book, then you disbelieve the words of Jesus himself because it is the basis of this writing.

SIGNS OF THE END TIMES

Pastors, evangelists, and Christian leaders around the world are seeing and speaking about the signs of the end times within today's current events.

Iniquity abounding:
We see traditional morals becoming less accepted, and new anti-biblical morals being introduced. Examples of this are; the immoral and grossly unfair behavior of, abortion of babies, homosexual behavior, persecution of religious beliefs, the watering down of the Word of God, and the lack of empathy and feelings, as well as prayer, bibles and God taken from our schools, work areas, political platforms and courtrooms.

Not only is the LBGT community being accepted, but also the new movement of, Pedophile-ism which is being introduced on the LBGT coat tail, with their slogan "Love is love". No one has obviously read Lev. 18:22-24, or Deut. 23:1 have they?

Don't get me started on the allowing of adult and/or child to choose the sexual preference they want to be, and/or their parents choosing for them and paying for the operations.

Rise of false prophets and false teachings:
For this one I want to focus on one particular one called the QAnon. This is a alternative religion that is cleverly and rapidly invading churches, taking on power of a new religion, that's causing division within the church. This is step one in the deceit and the great fallen away Det. 18:20-22; Matt. 7:15; 24:24; Mark 7:6-9; Rom. 16:18; II Cor. 11:13-15; II Tim. 4:3; II Pet. 2:1; I John 4:1-6.

Earthquakes in diverse places:
Currently we have seen, earthquakes in diverse places, fires burning rapidly, and other natural disasters shredding across the world. This is not a coincidence, this is spoken of within the Bible about end time signs Matt. 24:7; Luke 21:11

Other signs:
World conflicts among nations. Not only have we seen conflicts in the Middle East, but we have seen man made pestilence *Coronavirus* which has caused other conflicts, such as trade wars. These issues are rapidly leading toward world economic collapse, and the fall of society, which In turn will lead toward a one world government, closely followed by the mark of the beast.

This mark of the beast is already in progress, Bill Gates has been testing both a rice size chip as well as a tattoo style mark, both which seem to work. What better way to push this across the world, then cleverly disguising it as proof of a vaccine. Consider this, if any vaccine is required with such a thing to be placed on or in the wrists, hands or head, I would stand clear of this mark of damnation. This is step 2 in the deceit and great fallen away.

I believe that the end times is nigh. We are closer than you may think. On 13 August 2020, Israel, who met behind close doors with the United Arab Emirates (UAE), gave the ground breaking news of a peace treaty. UAE who is seen as the leadership front of the entire Arabic world, has issued a invoking to all Arab nations to follow suite. Is this the conferment behind close doors and the peace treaty the Bible talks about? Or is this the pre-cursor to? Only time will tell.

This is why we must look for the signs as stated in the Bible so we are not caught off guard, and he does not come like a thief in the night.

Not long after all this, we the elect of God will be persecuted and hunted down as enemies of the state. Which we will talk more of within the next few chapters of this book.

JOHN'S LETTERS TO THE SEVEN CHURCHES

Regardless of the different views and beliefs of Revelation, a majority can agree that the first three chapters of Revelation are, introduction of the Almighty God, and historical chapters about Johns letters to the first-century churches. Although some of these churches do not exist today, they still remain as a symbol to the modern churches that do exist. Some churches even fall under more than one letter written by John. One thing for sure today, is that many churches that exist are only here to tickle our ear with pleasant teachings versus the truths that are more difficult to hear that may be necessary to our salvation.

According to Rev. 1:11 on the Greek island of Patmos, Jesus Christ gave John seven messages and instructed him to: "…

what thou seest, write in a book, and send it unto the seven churches which are in Asia; unto Ephesus, and unto Smyrna, and unto Pergamos, and unto Thyatira, and unto Sardis, and unto Philadelphia, and unto Laodicea.

Jesus dictated a special message for each of the seven churches. The seven embedded messages follow a common pattern. Jesus began by introducing and describing himself, often with terms from Rev. 1. This compelled the assemblies to consider their actions in the light of who Jesus was. After stating that he knew their deeds or circumstances, Christ presented each church with a commendation except for Laodicea, a rebuke except for Smyrna and Philadelphia, an exhortation, and a promise to those who conquer evil. Although each message describes the historical situation of a first-century congregation, each message concludes with a universal call to hear what the spirit says to the churches.[vii]

To Ephesus Rev. 2:1-7, the loveless church. The church of Ephesus had many positive qualities in which Christ commended them by saying - they were dynamic, dedicated, determined, disciplined, and discerning Rev. 2:2-3.

In verse 4, Jesus brings out the rebuke "Nevertheless I have somewhat against thee, because thou hast left thy first love." Everything looked good about the Ephesus church on the outside, but the reality was that they had a heart issue. Their devotion to Christ diminished.[viii]

If you have found yourself in this place in your relationship with Christ, the following may help you to be restored 'to your first love'.

1. "Remember therefore from whence thou art fallen…" Rev. 2:5. If we have left something or someone, we must first remember where we started and realize where we are now.
2. After we remember where we started and realize where we are now, we are to "…repent…" Rev. 2:5.
3. Repeating the original good works will help you get back to where you began. "…and do the first works…" Rev. 2:5. Returning to what you did when you first became a Christian - the spiritual disciplines that kept you close to Christ and motivated you, will be what helps you to return to your first love and follow Him, again.

To Smyrna Rev. 2:8-11, the suffering church. Churches in the world think very little about being persecuted for their faith. But everyday there are churches around the world that face persecution on a daily basis. This was the case for the ancient church of Smyrna. They suffered because of pressure, poverty and persecution Rev. 2:9. Christ's letter to this church can prepare all believers for what is to come.

1. Be Fearless; "Fear none of those things which thou shalt suffer..." Rev. 2:10. Because Christ is always with us and is the one who controls all that is around us, we have nothing to fear. Christ's love for us is so great that "...tribulation...distress...persecution... famine...height...depth...nor any other creature, shall be able to separate us from the love of God..." Rom. 8:35-39.
   Fear is a natural response to what we cannot control, but with the Holy Spirit we have the power to live supernatural lives.
2. Be faithful; "...be thou faithful unto death, and I will give thee a crown of life." Rev. 2:10. Due to the intense persecution the Smyrna church suffered, I believe Christ was saying in this verse, "Yes, in My Name you will lose your life, but remain faithful to the very end."

To Pergamos Rev. 2:12-17, the compromising church. Pergamos was a city filled with pagan beliefs and practices and was better known as "Satan's City". Because of the pressure of the majority belief the church of Pergamos had compromised their faith by adding pagan beliefs as well as idolatry.

Satan still employs this strategy he used in Pergamos, "What you can't curse or crush, you can corrupt through compromise".

Christians should always speak truth in love Eph. 4:15, never being combative or antagonistic. We need to be vigilant, sober, and on-guard from corruption and compromise trying to take a foothold in the church. Therefore, the simple unvarnished truth needs to be spoken. Doing so is the way to avoid error. We must guard against the dilution of true doctrine by false teaching. If that makes us intolerant in the eyes of some, then so be it. Christ will commend us for it, just as he did "...Antipas...faithful martyr..." Rev. 2:13.

To Thyatira Rev. 2:19-29, the adulterous church. There are churches today who feel that their moral and spiritual boundaries should be closely connected and all-inclusive with each other. What this means is, that regardless of beliefs or whom they believe in, everyone is seeking a higher power that we call God.

The Pope Francis in 2019 made a push for inter-faith cooperation in his visit to the Arabian Peninsula.

He met with the Grand Imam and they signed a document promoting inter-faith dialogue, religious freedom and peace. During his visit, the Pope said that "...religious tolerance and freedom is the future...".

This is the start of the one world religion adulterous church. "...Jezebel, which calleth herself a prophetess, to teach and to seduce my servants to commit fornication immoralities. What does Christ say to a church that tolerates immorality in her midst?

1. The threat of distress; "Behold, I will cast her into a bed, and them that commit adultery with her into great tribulation, except they repent of their deeds." Rev. 2:22. Christ is given the church a chance to repent, or else they will face His great judgement.
2. The threat of death; "And I will kill her children with death..." Rev. 2:23. The warning was not just to the prophetess, but also to those members of the church who committed adultery with her.
3. The message to the Christians; "...as many as have not this doctrine, and which have not known the depths of Satan, as they speak; I will put upon you none other burden. But that which ye have already hold fast till I come." Rev. 2:24-25. This message

is for those who stood their ground and remained faithful to Christ by not engaging in immoralities.

4. The message to the conquerors; "And he that overcometh, and keepeth my works unto the end, to him will I give power over the nations: And he shall rule them with a rod of iron…And I will give him the morning star." Rev. 2:26-28. This message is for those who remained faithful to Christ. He promised them to be "caught-up" and they would reign with Christ.

To Sardis Rev. 3:1-6, The dead church. Though filled with external works and activity, this church is known as the dead church. As Paul puts it "Having a form of godliness, but denying the power thereof: from such turn away." II Tim 3:5.

Because of their failure to walk with the Lord, they were denying the real power of God through hypocrisy.[ix] This was a church full of what we call today "nominal Christians" or Christians in name only. Christ gives four specific directions for the church that is dead.

1. Be sensitive to sin; "Be watchful, and strengthen the things which remain…" Rev. 3:2. This warning conveys the idea of chasing away sleep. In other words, stay alert. As the Apostle Paul wrote "…awake thou

that sleepest, and arise from the dead, and Christ shall give thee light." Eph. 5:14.

2. Be submissive to the Holy Spirit; Christ charges the church to, "Remember therefore how thou hast received and heard…" Rev. 3:3. He is referring to the importance of the Holy Spirit. It is the power of the Holy Spirit that enables us to engage our sinful culture from a position of redemption and receive the word of God in a life changing way.[x]
3. Be subject to the authority of God's word in the church. The next instruction to Sardis is to hold "… Hold fast…" Rev. 3:3, which means 'to keep". It is used four other times in the book of Revelation in referencing to keeping the word of God Rev. 1:3; 3:8; 12:17 and 22:7. Christ charges his people to know the Word of God and obey it. We must allow it to govern our corporate and personal lives. This is meant through the lives of our churches and the lives of individuals within our churches. Hiding Gods word in our hearts is the key to avoiding temptations. This should be the foundation for our choices and actions.
4. Repent. Christ's final charge to the church of Sardis is "…repent…" Rev. 3:3. It's pretty simple, we repent or we suffer the consequences for living a life of ungodliness.

To Philadelphia Rev. 3:7-13, the faithful church. Christ commended the church of Philadelphia for four things.

"I know thy works: behold, I have set before thee an open door, and no man can shut it: for thou hast little strength, and thou hast kept my word, and hast not denied my name." Rev. 3:8.

If we want to be commended like the church of Philadelphia, we must go through open doors of ministry, depend upon Christs strength, be true to his word and never deny him. What does this mean for Christs saints?

1. The open door. This weak but faithful church needs assurance that God has power to bring about his sovereign will. If the Holy Spirit flows within the church and the church is committed to Christ, there will be many open doors to ministries that will connect Christ to our community. The church should pray for those doors to be seen, opened and walked through.
2. Little Strength. Churches today look at their size or numbers within and believe that they are too few to accomplish God's will. Excuses are used such as, there is too little money, too few gifts and not enough opportunities. Remember that when we are weak or

little, Christ is strong and big. Building the church is not up to us, it is up to Christ. We need to listen, support and help our shepherds that Christ has given us, to give his body the strength it needs.

3. Keeping Gods word. Being faithful and true to God's word and depending on Christ's strength will open doors of ministry. When the Word of God is the first priority, everything else will fall into place.
4. Not denying Christ. Because the church is so badly to identify with Christ regardless of the cost. We must remember that persecution grows the church. It is a quality of endurance. When things get tough, the church learns to get innovative. We learn how to reach others. We must proclaim, "Neither is there salvation in any other: for there is none other name under heaven given among men, whereby we must be saved." Acts 4:12.

To Laodicea Rev. 3:14-22, The lukewarm church. The church of Laodicea was lacking in every way possible. It was a wretched, miserable, poor, blind and naked church. Christ said, "So then because thou art lukewarm, and neither cold nor hot, I will spue thee out of my mouth." Rev. 3:16. The modern churches should take note; those words may apply to our church as well. When your complacent, you become lukewarm to spiritual things, proud of your accomplishments and arrogant in your ways. We would be advised to apply this counsel to our lives and our churches today. What is the prescription for such churches?

1. They need to buy riches of God; If the church is going to experience zeal instead of complacency, the riches of God must have priority over the riches of the world. Christ said, "Lay not up for yourselves treasures upon the earth, where moth and rust doth corrupt, and where thieves break through and steal:" Matt. 6:19. It is too tempting to focus our attention upon less important things instead of focusing on God.
2. They need to be clothed in white cloths to cover their nakedness; If the church is going to experience zeal instead of complacency, we must cover our nakedness. Throughout the scriptures there are many places that white cloths are symbols of God's acceptance and the true righteousness that comes from a born-again relationship with Jesus, which covers our spiritual nakedness.
    a. "But seek ye first the kingdom of God, and his righteousness; and all these things shall be added unto you." Matt. 6:33.
    b. Righteousness does not happen overnight it is a lifelong process.

c. A good business will tell you, in quality-control they are not concerned about the product, they are concerned about the process. If the process is right the product is guaranteed.
   1. How relevant is that to our Christianity?
   2. We tend to be more oriented with the product then with the process.
   3. As Christians we tend to desire and demand products of righteousness, but we give little attention to the process of righteousness. When it comes to righteousness process is everything.

3. They need to "…anoint thine eyes with eye salve…" Rev. 3:18, so they can see; If the church is going to experience zeal instead of complacency we must live in an active and strong relationship with Jesus.
   a. Laodicea was the center of a flourishing medical school which was noted for its eye ointment. One of the great diseases of the ancient world was infections of the eye that brought about blindness. The ointment made at Laodicea was a remedy greatly sought after by the world.
   b. The Christians of Laodicea lived life safely; they neither denied Christ nor themselves. This is what made them lukewarm. As to live for Christ

is to deny thyself and the things of the world. reference?

c. Too often we become satisfied with our current spiritual condition and we lose sight of the really important things of the Christian faith, such as faith, obedience, praise, worship and Christ-likeness, which produce true righteousness.
d. Instead, we settle for a life lived by rules and regulations or religious rites that become a substitute for true spiritual liveliness.

The things Jesus says to this church are harsh because he loves them and earnestly desires to be with them.

"As many as I love, I rebuke and chasten: be zealous therefore, and repent. Behold, I stand at the door, and knock: if any man hear my voice, and open the door, I will come in to him, and will sup with him, and he with me." Rev. 3:19-20. Jesus would have them repent of their complacency and become zealous for him.

Have you seen your own spiritual condition illustrated by this church? If so then you need to repent and become zealous for Christ.

Churches become lukewarm, proud and arrogant when the members become lukewarm, proud and arrogant.

SETTING THE SCENE

In the previous chapter we looked at John's letter to the seven churches, which was the present for John, and is history to us. However, the letters still represent churches and Christians of today. We enter Revelation chapter 4 where John starts with, "After this I looked, and, behold, a door was opened in heaven: and the first voice which I heard was as it were of a trumpet talking with me; which said, come up hither, and I will shew thee things which must be hereafter." Rev. 4:1.

As John enters heaven, he tries to describe what can hardly be put into words. Everything he describes is centered around an enormous throne. He talks of the one sitting on the throne to be, "...like a jasper and sardine stone: and there was a rainbow around the throne, in sight like unto an emerald." Rev. 4:3. The one sitting on the throne is assumed to be God.

John goes on to describe what he saw around the throne. "And around about the throne were four and twenty seats: and upon the seats I saw four and twenty elders sitting, clothed in white raiment; and they had on their heads crowns of gold." Rev. 4:4.

Elders indicate that they are human and not angels. This also is a representation of the items promised by Jesus to those who overcome in the church: a white garment Rev. 3:5, a crown Rev. 2:10; 3:11, and a throne Rev. 3:21.

The crowns the elders wear are not king's crowns but victor's crowns as promised throughout the New Testament to Christians who faithfully follow Jesus.[xi]

John explains that surrounding the throne, "...was a sea of glass like unto crystal..." Rev. 4:6, this sea of glass was to reflect and magnify the mighty light of God.

"...In the midst of the throne, and round about the throne, were four beasts full of eyes before and behind. And the first beast was like a lion, and the second beast like a calf, and the third beast had a face as a man, and the fourth beast was like a flying eagle. And the four beasts had each of them six wings about him; and they were full of eyes within...".

These are, Cherubim/cherubs, which are angelic beings involved in the worship and praise of God. The cherubim are first mentioned in the Bible in Gen. 3:24. "After He drove the man out, He placed on the east side of the Garden of Eden cherubim and a flaming sword flashing back and forth to guard the way to the tree of life." Prior to his rebellion, Satan was a cherub Ezek. 28:12-15. John ends chapter 4 with the Cherubs and elders worshipping and praising God, as well as himself giving God all the praise and glory.

In Revelation chapter 5, John sees another vision which he records. "And I saw in the right hand of him that sat on the throne a book written within and on the backside, sealed with seven seals." Rev. 5:1. John hears an angel proclaiming that no one on earth, living or dead, is worthy to break the seals of the book. John begins to weep until one of the elders told John to, "…weep not: behold, the lion of the tribe of Juda, the Root of David, hath prevailed to open the book, and to loose the seven seals thereof." Rev. 5:5. This Lion of Juda and Root of David was Jesus; The Lamb that, "...wast slain, and hast redeemed us to God by the Blood out of every kindred, and tongue, and people, and nation;" Rev. 5:9. John then heard the voice of many angels, the beasts and the elders round about the throne giving all blessing, honor, glory and power to him that sitteth on the throne and to the Lamb forevermore. "And the four beasts said Amen. And the four and twenty elders fell down and worshipped him that for ever and ever." Rev. 5:14.

John is not only permitted to gaze into heaven through an open door, he is also invited to pass through that door and enter into heaven. The invitation is not issued for the sake of satisfying his curiosity. He is summoned so that he may learn about "the things that must be hereafter" the events that must take place in history and in the world before the coming of the Lord Jesus Christ.

> Note: The actual revelation of these things is not given until chapter 6 of Revelation; but because of the nature of these events that involve tribulation for the world and for the church, it is essential that the apostle and the church be prepared to handle them, that is why John is granted the two visions recorded in Rev. 4 and 5:12.[xii]

THE FIRST FIVE SEALS

In Revelation chapter 6 we are just getting into the opening of the seals, of the book the Lamb had in chapter 5. These seals are to be opened before Jesus descends in like manner that he ascended into heaven. This is where we start getting into the meat and potatoes of Revelation and the End Time Prophecy. Everything leading up to this point has pretty much been an introduction. This section begins with the opening of the first four seals, which release four colored horses Zech. 1:8-11; 6:1-7 bringing conquest, war, scarcity, and death.[xiii]

The first four seals are what many call the four horsemen of the apocalypse unveiling. The word apocalypse comes from the Greek word apokalupsis, meaning disclosure or revelation. Thus, the four horsemen of the apocalypse, means the four horsemen of revelation.

In Rev. 6:1-2, the first of the seven seals being opened, "And I saw the Lamb opened one of the seals, and I heard, as it were the noise of thunder, one of the four beasts saying, Come and see. And I saw, and behold a white horse: and he that sat on him had a bow; and a crown was given unto him: and he went forth conquering, and to conquer." Here we are introduced to a rider on a white horse which appears to use diplomacy and a promise of peace to establish a one-world government.

Comparing the seals to the events Christ said would happen in His famous Olivet prophecy, this seal represents religious deception and the false prophets Jesus foretold about in that prophecy Matt. 24:5. They will pretend to be ministers of the gospel, but in fact are wolves in sheep's clothing. Remember Satan, and his fallen angels, can appear to be preachers of righteousness II Cor. 11:15.

The first seal allows the Antichrist to come into the world riding a white horse and wearing a crown, which symbolizes that the Antichrist will promote peace and holds great power in the world. This makes sense as he who is a false-Christ will come in on a white horse impersonating Christ in the way he, himself, comes as the righteous rider in Rev. 19:11.

In Rev. 6:3-4, "And when he had opened the second seal, I heard the second beast say, Come and see. And there went out another horse that was red: and power was given to him that sat thereon to take peace from the earth, and they would kill one another: and there was given unto him a great sword." The second seal introduces us to peace being taken from the earth. The one who rides the red horse is given the authority to make war. Just when peace was brought by the white horse, another comes and sweeps it away. War will rule the world.

In Rev. 6:5-6, "And when he had opened the third seal, I heard the third beast say, Come and see. And I beheld, and lo a black horse; and he that sat on him had a pair of balances in his hand. And I heard a voice in the midst of the beasts say, a measure of wheat for a penny, and three measures of barley for a penny; and see thou hurt not the oil and wine." The third seal, is where we see the prices of food being brought out. The suffering of famine due to inflation is caused by the aftermath of the war. The Beast will soon reveal the plan to solve the famine through a mark to be taken.

In Rev. 6:7-8, "And when he opened the fourth seal the forth seal, I heard the voice of the fourth beast say, Come and see. And I looked, and behold a pale horse: and his name that sat on him was Death, and hell followed with him. And power was given unto them over the fourth part of the earth, to kill with sword, and with hunger, and with death, and with the beasts of the earth." This is when death is released and one-quarter of the world's population, both man and creature, will be killed.

This massive death toll is reached with famine, pestilence and by the wild beasts of the earth.[xiv] Note here in verse 8 it said, "…and power was given unto them…", this is the Antichrist that is described in chapter 13 of Revelation.

In Rev. 6:9-11, "And when he had opened the fifth seal, I saw under the alter the souls of them that were stained for the word of God, and for the testimony which they held: And they cried with a loud voice, saying, how long, oh Lord, holy and true, dost thou not judge and avenge our blood on them that dwell on the earth? And white robes were given unto every one of them; and it was said unto them, that they should rest yet for a little season, until their fellow servants also and their brethren, that should be killed as they were, should be fulfilled." This is the fifth seal, where John looks into heaven and sees the souls of the martyrs, calling out for judgment and to be avenged. They were murdered for their allegiance to the word of God and their testimony of Jesus Christ. They were told to wait a little longer as they wait for their brothers who is to be killed as they were. These are those Christians that have been killed in all of history for their belief in Christ. Let us compare to what other books of the Bible has to say, and show just how much there is a sequence of events that is to take place and the order they are supposed to happen. In Matthew 24, Mark 13 and Luke 21 etc., the following events which follow the seals exactly as they are listed, as told by Jesus;

1. 1st seal found in Matt. 24:4-5; Mark 13:5-6, and Luke 21:8, II Thess. 2:3
2. 2nd seal found in Matt. 24:7, Mark13:7-8 and Luke 21:9-10
3. 3rd seal found in Matt. 24:7; Mark13:8 and Luke 21:11
4. 4th seal found in Matt. 24:7; Mark13:8 and Luke 21:11
5. 5th seal found in Matt. 24:9-10; Mark 13:9; 11-13; Luke 21:12 and 16-17

Do you see the order and how they remain the same?

Before the abomination of desolation, the Antichrist receives a fatal blow to one of its heads, causing death. This deadly wound will be miraculously healed and many will wonder after the head who is now the beast, and many are in awe at his miraculous resurrection.

If we look into Rev. 13:1-2 the dragon gives the Beast power and authority. This sets himself up to claim he is the long-awaited messiah, and he will declare war upon the Saints of God.

DAYS OF YESHUA

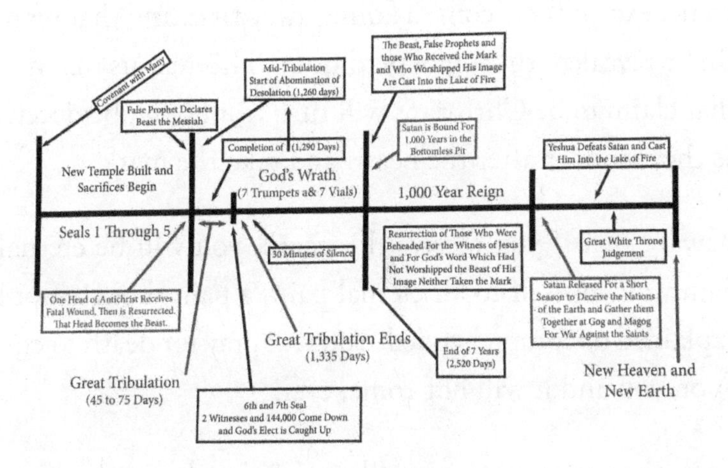

Leading up to the abomination of desolation Christians will see persecution, but these will intensify upon completion of the abomination of desolation, which so begins the great tribulation period of approximately 45-75 days as told to us in the book of Dan. 12:11-12.

At the Abomination of Desolation Dan. 9:27; 11:31; 12:11; Matt. 24:15; Mark 13:14, the false prophet will proclaim the beast as the messiah and will order images of the beast to be made and worshipped. If anyone refuses to worship the beast they will be killed Rev. 13:15. The beast will also require that all will receive a mark on their right hand or in their forehead. Without the mark they will not be able to buy, sell or trade Rev. 13:16-17.

The Bible tells us in II Thess. 2:3 ; "…that day shall not come, except there come a falling away first, and that man of sin be revealed, the son of perdition;" This tells us that many that claim to be Christians will turn from God, be deceived as they wonder after the beast, and take the mark.

Beware that if you receive this mark, you will be eternally damning yourself to an eternal pain, a pain that cannot be explained or comprehended. You will pray for death to come upon you and it will not come, ever.

God gives us a promise, "Blessed is he that waiteth, and cometh to the thousand three hundred and five and thirty days." Dan. 12:12; "…He that overcometh shall not be hurt of the second death." Rev. 2:11. If we continue to persevere and do Christ's work to the very end, even if that means our death which is only temporary, we will be eternally blessed with great riches that cannot be fathomed. This does not indicate material riches, but richness of eternal life without suffering, pain, and sorrow.

The abomination of desolation marks two things in Daniels 70th weeks: the mid-point of the seven years 1260 days, and the start of the Great Tribulation. It is unknown what point will be seen clearly. Will it be the start of the abomination of desolation 1260th day, or will it be the completion of the abomination of desolation 1290th day?

I ask this so you better understand, why I say the Great Tribulation will last approximately 45-75 days. During which, God's elect will be hunted down, persecuted and killed for their beliefs. "And except those days should be shortened, there should no flesh be saved: but for the elects sake those days shall be shortened." Matt. 24:22. What this is saying that if it was not for the short period of 45-75 days, then there would be no Christians left to "catch-up" when the great and terrible day of Yeshua arrives.

In Rev. 6:12-17, "and I had beheld when he had opened the sixth seal, and, lo, there was a great earthquake; and the sun became black as sackcloth of hair, and the moon became as blood; and the stars of heaven fell unto the earth, even as a fig tree casteth her intimacy figs, when she is shaken of a mighty wind. And the heaven departed as a scroll when it is rolled together; and every mountain and island were moved out of their places. And the kinds of the earth, and the great men, and the rich men, and the chief captains, and the mighty men, and every bondman, and every free man, hid themselves in the dens and in the rocks of the mountains; and said to the mountains and rocks, fall on us, and hide us from the face of him that sitteth on the throne, and from the wrath of the Lamb: for the great day of his wrath is come; who shall be able to stand?" This is the sixth seal. This launches a cosmic disruption as the heavens collapse leading to hysterical panic as the glorious Day of Yeshua arrives. The language strongly echoes Isa. 2:10-21.[xv] However, before the 'catching away' the Bible tells us in both Rev. 7:1-8 and 14:1-7, about 144,000 sealed in the foreheads with God's seal.

This seal, which has been used before in Ezek. 9, is to keep God's people safe from his wrath that is being poured out upon the earth.

Who are the 144,000? They are 12,000 from the 12 tribes of the children of Israel Israelites, not Jews but Israelites [for further info on this read II Sam.]. At least nine of these tribes no longer exist today or are blended so much that they cannot identify from which tribe they have descended. So where do these 144,000 come from then? They are old testament saints who have already died and are in heaven. These saints are, specifically and literally, men from the 12 original tribes of the children of Israel, whom have not been defiled with women virgins, deemed from among men, and are already in heaven.

Where is the proof? The proof is, "And I looked, and, lo, a Lamb stood on the mount Sion, and with him an hundred forty and four thousand, having his Father's name written in their foreheads." Rev. 14:1. This verse says they are with the Lamb Jesus on mount Sion Heavenly Jerusalem as depicted in Heb. 12:22.

As you continue to read, it also goes on to say that, "And they sung as it were a new song before the throne, and before the four beasts, and the elders: and no man could learn that song but the hundred and forty and four thousand, which were redeemed from earth." Rev. 14:3. This verse also says that they are in Heaven singing a song that only they could know.

Further, "And I saw another angel fly in the midst of heaven, having the everlasting gospel to preach unto them that dwell on the earth, and to every nation, and kindred, and tongue, and people." Rev. 14:6. This explains that they are given the gospel of Christ to go forth and preach upon the earth.

Still not convinced?

Let's just jump further forward in the timeline to Revelation chapter 9. "And there came out of the smoke locusts upon the earth: and unto them was given the power, as the scorpions of the earth have power. And it was commanded them that they should not hurt the grass of the earth, neither any green thing, neither any tree; but only those men which have not the seal of God in their foreheads." Rev. 9:3-4. This shows that the 144,000 are on the earth, during the wrath of God 7 Trumpets & 7 Vials, preaching the word of God.

Consider this, if the 144,000 are here preaching the Gospel, then does this mean there will be people who find salvation? Many will say no, 'because God takes away his Holy Spirit from this earth'. To those that agree with that, my rebuttal is this, where in the Bible does it say that the Holy Spirit is withdrawn from the earth?

I contend that the Bible does not say that the Holy Spirit will be withdrawn from the earth. If it will not, then it stands to reason that there will be some who find salvation during this time. They will be mortal not immortal, and they will be judged by their works, besides those who are killed for their belief in Christ. This will be explained later in the book.

As many hide in fear, God's elect will rejoice in this sight of Jesus's' coming, "and shall they see the Son of man coming in the clouds with great power and glory." Mark 13:26. This is the day they long awaited. This is the day of our catching away; the Day of Yeshua. "…we which are alive and remain unto the coming of the Lord shall not prevent them which are asleep. For the Lord himself shall descend from heaven with a shout, with the voice of the archangel, and with the trump of God: and the dead in Christ shall rise first: then we which are alive and remain shall be caught up together with them in the clouds, to meet the Lord in the air" I Thess. 4:15-17.

This is the point we all seek to reach, the day of Yeshua. The moment in which we are Caught-up to be with our Lord. Our Gods elect Judgement day.

Then comes the seventh seal: "And when they had opened the seventh seal, there was silence in heaven about the space of half an hour." Rev. 8:1 half an hour is not as we know it to be.

ONE MINUTE AFTER MIDNIGHT

King David said, "At midnight I will rise to give thanks unto thee because of the righteous judgements." Ps. 119:62. David is clearly saying that one minute after midnight, he will be in heaven looking down and rejoicing as God lays down his righteous judgements upon the Earth.

Those that are ready will be taken at the stroke of midnight Day of Yeshua. Those who are not will be left to witness and feel God's wrath upon the Earth. The elect that were ready and taken, will receive their judgement by being 'caught up' during the Day of Yeshua. Those that are not taken, will face judgement based upon their works. Would you rather be ready and taken during the day of Yeshua, then see that the Lord catch me by surprise like a thief in the night? I do not want to worry if my works will suffice to the Lord at the time of my judgement. I want to be ready when He comes.

Many movies, novels and books on the market today give false teaching of a secret reaping, the "Rapture", an event that they portray as one that will leave people wondering what happened to all those who have disappeared. It is portrayed that many will blame it on a weapon created by another country, until they see that they too were affected. The blame will be focused on some extraterrestrial invasion. Satan wants you to think that will happen.

In fact, many places in the Bible confirms that the day of reaping is in fact is no secret, and will not take place in secret. The day of reaping begins with the sun being darkened, the moon not giving off her light, and heaven and earth will be shaken, then shall everyone see Jesus coming in the clouds Mark 13:26-27. In Acts 1:11, the Evangelist Luke forewarns us, "…ye men of Galilee, why stand ye gazing unto heaven?

This same Jesus, which is taken up from you into heaven, shall so come in like manner as ye have seen him go into heaven.". To surmise, on this day it will be known who came for those that were taken. Those that believed not, will hide their selves in fear and/or shame.

At one minute after midnight Day of Yeshua, many who thought their selves to be worthy of God's grace and love, will find themselves looking to the sky in disbelief. They will all have the same questions:

> "What did I do?"
> "What did I not do?"
> "Why was I left behind?"
> "Were my works not good enough?"
> "Was my money not enough?"
> "Why did I not listen?"
> "Why has God forsaken me?"

"For the time will come when they will not endure sound doctrine; but after their own lusts shall they heap to themselves teachers, having itching ears; and they shall turn away their ears from the truth, and shall be turned unto fables." II Tim. 4:3-4. The sign talked about in this verse, have definitely been fulfilled in today's generation. A majority of professing Christians these days, do not read the word of God themselves, but rely upon their pastors, evangelists and prophet's word as truth. The Bible tells us to not believe everything we are taught, because not every teacher is from God. They may be a false prophet I John 4:1. We must read Gods word and pray daily, not solely relying on what we hear.

There will great blame laid upon many religious church leaders, for the many that knew not the truth because of their false teachings. Many churches today are being led by false prophets, who take and teach what they want from the bible, and discards what they don't want. These false prophets are motivational speakers that teach "tickle my ear sermons", because they want the numbers in attendance, and want to be popular.

They refuse to teach the "hard to hear sermons", that speak the hard truth in love, and that tell us that if we don't change our ways we will surely go to hell.

The Bible is filled of verses that tell us to beware of false teachers and prophets, who will act and talk as a lamb, but will in fact be a wolf in sheep clothing Matt. 7:15. These false teachers and prophets will be Satan's followers, for they knowingly know the true path and true teachings but choose to follow the wrong path and deceive their followers, leading them to their destruction.

These false prophets, teachers and churches are and will feed the majority with cardinal things, changing the church to societies norms, and saying that things like; idolatry, adultery, violence, lust, greed, disrespect, homosexuality, theft, lying, aggression, selfishness.

Iniquity has truly abounded, as many Christian churches are full of unconverted, sin loving people. Many of them believe that they can continue living in sin, as long as they ask for forgiveness, "believe" in Jesus and attend church weekly on Sunday or whatever their churches day of worship is. These churches are not properly feeding their sheep that are truly seeking Christ, they are in fact starving them.

The papers, magazines and news agencies will want to be the first to give the headlines. They already have the headlines laid out. I don't want to be here to hear it or read it. Do you? Where will you find yourself 1 minute after midnight? Will you be gazing up to the sky, your mind filled with questions, wondering why he came this day? Will you be with Yeshua?

29 minutes later, ye shall see Gods wrath…

GOD'S WRATH

Up to this point the world was experiencing Satan's wrath upon the earth and against the saints of God. Now we transition to see God's wrath being poured upon all the earth for their sins against God and his people.

In Rev. 8:7, "The first angel sounded, and there followed hail and fire mingled with blood, and they were cast upon the earth: and the third part of the trees was burnt up, and all green grass was burnt up.", this is the First Trumpet of Gods Wrath, which destroys a third of the earth by fire and ravages the rest with hail.

In Rev. 16:2, "And the first went, and poured out his vial upon the earth; and there fell a noisome and grievous sore upon the men which had the mark of the beast, and upon them which worshipped his image.", This is the First Vial of

Gods Wrath, here we witness a sore that plagues those that bear the beasts mark, with nerve racking pain.

In Rev. 8:8-9, "And the second angel sounded, and as it were a great mountain burning with fire was cast into the sea: and the third part of the sea became blood; and the third part of the creatures which were in the sea, and had life, died; and the third part of the ships were destroyed.", this was the Second Trumpet of Gods Wrath, and at this point we will witness Gods trumpets and vials coming together.

In Rev. 16:3, "And the second angel poured out his vial upon the sea; and it became as the blood of a dead man: and every living soul died upon the sea.", this is the Second Vial of Gods Wrath. And we now see the Trumpets and Vials are in the same form, this one in particular, we see Gods wrath covering the sea and the sea life.

In Rev. 8:10-11, "And the third angel sounded, and there fell a great star from heaven, burning as it were a lamp, and it fell upon the third part of the rivers, and upon the fountains of waters; and the name of the star is called wormwood: and the third part of the waters became wormwood; and many men died of the waters, because they were made bitter.", this was the Third Trumpet of Gods Wrath.

In Rev. 16:4-7, "And the third angel poured out his vial upon the rivers and fountains of waters; and they became blood. And I heard the angel of the waters say, thou art righteous O Lord, which art, and wast, and shalt be, because thou hast judged us. For they have shed the blood of saints and prophets, and thou hast given them blood to doing; for they are worthy. And I heard another out of the altar say, even so, Lord God Almighty, true and righteous are thy judgements.", this is the Third Vial of Gods Wrath. Again the Trumpets and Vials are in the same form, this being now upon the rivers and fountains of waters, in which the waters are made bitter.

In Rev. 8:12, "And the fourth angel sounded, and the third part of the sun was smitten, and the third part of the moon, and the third part of the stars; so as the third part of them was darkened, and the day shone not for a third part of it, and the night likewise.", This is the Fourth Trumpet of Gods Wrath.

In Rev. 16:8-9, "And the fourth angel poured out his vial upon the sun; and the power was given unto him to scorch men with fire. And men were scorched with great heat, and blasphemed the name of God, which have power over these plagues: And they repented not to give him glory.", This is the Fourth Vial of Gods Wrath. We still see the Trumpets and Vials being for the most part in the same form, this being sun. "And I beheld, and heard an angel flying through the midst of heaven, saying with a loud voice, Woe, woe, woe, to the inhabiters of the earth by reason of the other voices of the trumpet of the three angels, which are yet to sound." Rev. 8:13.

The last three Trumpets and Vials are the three woes to come, which echo Isaianic woe judgements. Isa. 3:9-11; 5:8-22 and underscores the shock, horror, and anguish of the fifth, sixth, and seventh trumpets.[xvi]

In Rev. 9:1-6, "the fifth angel sounded, and I saw a star fall from heaven unto the earth: and to him was given the key to the bottomless pit. And he opened the bottomless pit; and there arose a smoke out of the pit, as the smoke of a great furnace; and the sun and the air were darkened by reason of the smoke of the pit. And there came out of the smoke locusts upon the earth: and unto them was given power, as the scorpions of the earth have power. And it was commanded them that they should not hurt the grass of the earth, neither any green thing, neither any tree, but only those men which have not the seal of God in their foreheads. And to them it was given that they should not kill them, but that they should be tormented five months: and their torment was as the torment of a scorpion, when he strikers a man. And in those days shall men desire to die, and death shall flee from them."

> Note: The star that falls from heaven is the Angel in charge of the bottomless pit whom in Hebrew is named Abandon and in Greek is known as Apollyon, that we later see in chapter 20 as the one who bounds Satan up and casts him into the bottomless pit for a thousand years. This is the fifth Trumpet of Gods Wrath.

In Rev. 16:10-11, "And the fifth angel poured out his vial upon the seat of the beast; and his kingdom was full of darkness; and they gnawed their tongues for pain, And Blasphemed the God of heaven because of their pains and their sores, and repented not of their deeds." This is the fifth vial of Gods wrath. We continue to see the Trumpets and Vials in the same form, this bringing darkness upon the earth and great suffering and pain from their sores, and the sting given unto them.

In Rev. 9:12, "One Woe is past; and, behold, there come two Woes more hereafter."

In Rev. 9:13-21, "And the sixth angel sounded, and I heard a voice from the four horns of the golden altar which is before

God, saying to the sixth angel which had the trumpet, loose the four angels which are bound in the great river Euphrates. And the four angels were loosed, which were prepared for an hour, and a day, and a month, and a year, for to slay a third part of men. And the number of the army of the horsemen were two hundred thousand: and I heard the number of them. And thus, I saw the horses in the vision, and them that sat on them, having breastplates of fire, and of Jacinth, and brimstone: and the heads of the horses were as heads of lions; and out of their mouths issued fire and smoke and brimstone. By these three was a third part of men killed, by the fire, and by the smoke, and by the brimstone, which issued out of their mouths. For their power is in their mouth, and in their tails: for their tails were like unto serpents, and had heads, and with them they do hurt. And the rest of the men which were not killed by these plagues yet repented not of the works of their hands, that they should not worship devils, and idols of gold, and silver, and brass, and stone, and wood: which neither can see, nor hear, nor walk: Neither repented they of their murders, nor of their sorceries, nor of their fornication, nor of their thefts." This is the sixth Trumpet of Gods Wrath.

In Rev. 16:12-16, "And the sixth angel poured out his vial upon the great river Euphrates; and the water thereof was dried up, that the way of the kings of the east might be prepared. And I saw three unclean spirits like frogs come out of the mouth of the beast, and out of the mouth of the false prophet. For they are spirits of devils, working miracles, which go forth unto the kings of the earth and of the whole world, to gather them to battle of that great day of God almighty. Behold, I come as a thief. Blessed is he that watcheth, and keepeth his garments, lest he walk naked, and they see his shame. And he gathered them together into a place called in the Hebrew tongue Armageddon." This is the sixth vial of Gods wrath.

As we continue to see the Trumpets and Vials as the same form, the sixth dries up the Euphrates and releases the four angels bound within it to prepare for the great war of Armageddon.

Now on to one of the most extraordinary and unusual of all of the recorded testimonies in the Apocalypse and of all of the things that are revealed in the Word of God. Everything about it is unusual and extraordinary. For example, there was never in record any two witnesses like these two. There is never portrayed in any story, in Biblical or secular literature anything comparable to the record that is made here of these two prophets of God.

There are many martyrs slain under the reign of the beast, but none of them receive the attention that is given to these two remarkable and unusual witnesses. Another unusual thing about it; all the visions in the Revelation John sees, he looks at them, and he writes them down. He hears the characters speak, and he writes down what they say—all except this one instance. John doesn't't see these two witnesses. They're not presented to him in a vision. "And the angel which I saw stand upon the sea and upon the earth lifted up his hands to heaven." Rev. 10:5. It is that angel of our Lord who tells John about these two witnesses. John does not see them. The angel tells him about them and describes them and their course of ministry in the earth Rev. 11:1-13.

Another unusual and remarkable thing about this passage: evidently, most evidently, they are living here in a time and an era after grace altogether different from the age and the time of love and grace and forgiveness in which we are now living. Look at these two prophets. "And if any man will hurt them, fire proceedeth out their mouth, and devoureth their enemies: and if any man will hurt them, he must in this manner be killed." Rev. 11:5. That is the exact opposite of everything that we are taught in this present spirit and age of mercy and grace. Our Lord said:

> "But I say unto you which hear, love your enemies, do good to them which hate you, Bless them that curse you, and pray for the, which despitefully use you.
>
> And unto him that smiteth thee on the one cheek offer also the other; and him that taketh away thy cloak forbid not to take thy coat also." Luke 6:27-29.
>
> "And if any man will sue thee at the law, and take thy coat, let him have thy cloak also. And whosoever shall compel thee to go a mile, go with him twain." Matt. 5:40-41.

Our great apostle Paul said, "Dearly beloved, avenge not yourselves, but rather give place unto wrath: for it is written, vengeance is mine; I will repay, saith the Lord. Therefore, if thine enemy hunger, feed him; if he thirst, give him drink: for in doing so thou shalt heap coals of fire upon his head." Rom. 12:19-20.

That was exemplified in all of the testimony and witness of our Lord and of His apostles. There is no refusal on the part of God's apostles or of the Lord Himself who was crucified, to suffer at the hands of His enemies.

But this is an altogether different time, and different age Revelation speaks of. The two psalm that especially describe the passion of our Savior are Psalm 22 and 69. Both of the psalms at the beginning describe the sufferings of our Lord Ps. 22:1-21; 69:1-21, and both of the psalms are quoted as our Lord dies on the cross Matt. 27:46. But beginning at verse 22 in both of the psalms, the result of that death of our Lord is diametrically opposite Ps. 22:22; 69:22.

In Ps. 22, after the sufferings of our Lord are portrayed Ps. 22:1-21, beginning at verse 22 there are blessings, blessings, blessings that flow from His sacrifice, and they are portrayed here in verse after verse Ps. 22:22-31; all of the sweetness, and the goodness, and the praise, and the grace, and the forgiveness, and the love, and the mercies that flow from the sacrifice of our Lord. But when you turn to Psalm 69 and begin at verse 22 there, oh, the curses and the judgments. Ps. 69:22-28.

When you get through describing the sufferings of our Lord at verse 21 of Psalm 69, "They gave Me also gall for My meat; and in My thirst they gave My vinegar to drink."; now when you get through describing the sufferings of our Lord, then comes judgment and vengeance upon His adversaries. Starting at verse 22:

- "Let their table become a snare before them"
  Ps. 69:22 ;
- "Let their eyes be darkened, that they see not"
  Ps. 69:23 ;
- "Pour out Thine indignation upon them, and let Thy wrathful anger take hold of them"
  Ps. 69:24 ;
- "Add iniquity unto their iniquity: and let them not come into Thy righteousness"
  Ps. 69:27 ;
- "Let them be blotted out of the book of the living, and not be written with the righteous"
  Ps. 69:28.

The thing that happens is very apparent. But, there is coming another day, and another hour, and another time, in which the man that has turned down the grace of God and the overtures of His love and mercy, when that man shall face the day of vengeance and of wrath and the judgment of the Almighty. Heb. 10:31. All these things make you tremble.

Another unusual and extraordinary thing about this revelation Rev. 11:1-13 ; you would think that so distinguished and unusual prophets and witnesses of Christ would be named. Who are they? They are unnamed, and not only that, but as I have read and read and read, and studied and studied and studied, I do not think there is any man that has ever lived who can identify these two witnesses. Oh, the attempts that are made to do it. Most of the interpreters will say they are Enoch and Elijah, and the reason they say that is because of one passage of Scripture.

Hebrews 9:27 says, "...It is appointed unto men once to die..." so, going back into the Old Testament Scriptures, they find that there are two men in the Old Testament Scriptures who never died. One was Enoch Gen. 5:24, and one was Elijah II Kings 2:11. They were taken up to heaven, ascending like the Lord.

And they believe just on the basis of that one passage that these two witnesses Rev. 11:3, are Enoch and Elijah who have come back to the earth, and here they are slain, and they die according to Heb. 9:27, that all men must die and face the judgment.

The generalization from that text is not true. All men are not going to die. We who are alive and remain to the coming of the Lord shall never taste of death I Thess. 4:15. just like that. We are all not going to die. The generation of believers who is living when our Lord shall come will never taste of death.

When you look at the passage, the miracles they are able to perform are characteristic of Moses and Elijah. They have "power to shut heaven that it rain not in the days of their prophecy," that sounds like Elijah I kings 17:1; James 5:17-18, and they have "...power over waters to turn them to blood and to smite the earth with all plagues as often as they will" Rev. 11:6 ; that sounds like Moses in the land of Egypt Exod. 8:19-20.

These men cannot be named. We do not know who they are. They are Moses-like and Elijah-like in their power. In the spirit and the might, in the anointing and unction from heaven of Moses and Elijah, these two witnesses stand in the earth, but who they are we do not know Rev, 11:3-4.

In Rev. 11:14, "The second Woe is past; and, behold, the third Woe cometh quickly."

In Rev. 11:15-19, "And the seventh angel sounded; and there were great voices in heaven, saying, the kingdoms of this world are become the kingdoms of our Lord, and of his Christ; and he shall ring for ever and ever.

And the four and twenty elders, which sat before God on their seats, fell upon their faces, and worshipped God, Saying, we give thee thanks, O Lord God Almighty, which art, and wast, and art to come; because thou hast taken to thee thy great power, and hast reigned.

And the nations were angry, and thy wrath is come, and the time of the dead, that they should be judged, and that thou shouldest give reward unto thy servants and prophets, and to the saints, and them that fear thy name, small and great; and shouldest destroy them which destroy the earth. And the temple of God was opened in heaven, and there was seen in his temple the ark of his testament: and there were lightnings, and voices, and thunderings, and an earthquake, and great hail." This is the seventh Trumpet of Gods Wrath.

In Rev. 16:17-21, "And the seventh angel poured out his vial into the air; and there came a great voice out of the temple of heaven, from the throne, saying, it is done. And their were voices, and thunders, and lightnings; and there was a great earthquake, such as was not since men were upon the earth, so mighty an earthquake, and so great. And the great city was divided into three parts, and the cities of the nations fell: and great Babylon came in remembrance before God, to give unto her the cup of the wine of the fierceness of his wrath. And every island fled away, and the mountains were not found. And there fell upon men a great hail out of heaven, every stone about the weight of a talent: and men blasphemed God because of the plagues of hail; for the plague thereof was exceeding great." This was the Seventh Vial of Gods Wrath.

And we see that in both the seventh Trumpet and Vial they are the same and end the Wrath of God in a great finale of voices, lightnings, thunderings, earthquake, and great hail that weighs approximately 75 lbs. Talent = 75 lbs. This was the great third Woe.

THE FALL OF THE BEASTS AND THE WHITE THRONE JUDGEMENT

Chapters 17-19 of Revelation is more of an "enlargement photograph" or a "hypertext window" that magnifies the catastrophic events of the 3rd woe 7th Trumpet & 7th Vial. This is explained in Rev. 17:1, "And there came one of the seven angels which had the seven vials, and talked with me, saying unto me, come hither; I will shew unto thee the judgement of the great whore that sitteth upon many waters:", Clearly this is another perspective of the wrath of God; the view of its catastrophic impact upon the prostitute.

The prostitute is the great city of Babylon that controls the kings of the earth. Basically the city is the center, capital and controller of the one-world government Anti-Christ, and the one-world religion lead by the false prophet. The false messiah beast controls the "entire network". In layman terms think of it as; President is the Beast, Cabinets of the government is the Anti-Christ, and the Religious advisor/ Pope/or Imam etc… is the False Prophet.

Therefore the kings of the earth, those who took the mark and those who worship the Beast have committed fornication against God Rev. 17:2, meaning they have been unfaithful and disloyal due unbelief and full of cardinal things. They have committed murder upon the saints Rev.17:6, and rejoiced with their death.

Revelation 17:10 says, "And there are seven kings: five are fallen, and one is, and the other is not yet come; and when he cometh, he must continue a short space.". Here we have the same idea as the previous verse in Rev.17:9, with a somewhat different aspect. The phrase in ver. 9, "seven mountains," regarded the world power as one universal indivisible whole, without respect to particular times or modes in which it might be exhibited.

In this phrase, "seven kings," we have the same world power viewed in its successive exhibitions by different nations; though here again we must be on our guard not to interpret the number seven literally of seven nations. The kings represent Worldly states or kingdoms; seven, again, betokens universality. We are thus told that this world power on which the woman relies is exhibited in the manifestation of power by successive nations, e.g. Egyptian, Assyrian, Roman, etc., as many as have ever existed or shall exist; for this is the meaning of seven. Five are fallen, and one is, and the other is not yet come; the five; the one; the other. Omit "and." Here, again, not literally five. The seer divides the whole series of antitheist world powers into three groups, and he would say, some, probably the majority, of these are passed away; the second group embraces the world power as it is exhibited now, whether Roman, Jewish, or any other; in the third group are included those yet to come.

Thus those writers who enumerate Egypt, Nineveh, Babylon, Persia, Greece, Syria, etc., in the first group, are partially correct, and only wrong in so far as they attempt to limit and define the kingdoms; and similarly also those who in the third group place the Roman empire after the barbarian invasions, or imperial Germany, etc. "...And when he cometh, he must continue a short space; a little while" Rev. 17:10. This "short space" describes the remainder of the time of the world's existence. Such is its meaning in Revelation 6:11 and Rev. 12:12, and again in Rev. 20:3. In a similar manner, also, "shortly come to pass," etc. Rev. 1:1; 3; Rev. 2:5; 16, etc.; also John 16:17; 28.[xvii]

The eighth being same as the seventh Rev.17:11 is the one whom revived the fatal blow, was resurrected and became the Beast False Messiah; however the eighth is the Beast overcome possessed by the dragon Satan himself. The dragon then gives power to ten kings over ten kingdoms to follow him into war against the Lamb Yeshua Rev. 17:12-14. God puts into the ten kings hearts to burn down the prostitute Babylon and destroy her and everything she stood for, fulfilling Gods will Rev. 17:16-17.

Revelation 18:8, "Therefore shall her plagues come in one day, death and mourning, and famine; and she shall be utterly burned with fire: for strong is the Lord God who judgeth her.". Keep in mind if a week equals seven years, then a day equals one year. Upon completion of the 3rd Woe, Heaven is opened and Christ who comes upon a white horse is followed by the armies of heaven; to make war against the Beast, the kings of the earth and their armies. The Beast is defeated and is cast with the false prophet, those who received his mark and they who worshipped his image, into the lake of fire Rev.19:11-21.

Then an angel falls to the earth; whom in Hebrew is named Abandon and in Greek is known as Apollyon, "...with the key to the bottomless pit and a great chain in his hand." Rev. 20:1. This Angel apparently having great strength grabs hold of Satan chains him up and casts him into the bottomless pit, sealing it for a period of a thousand years Rev. 20:2-3.

Those who were beheaded for the witness those who found salvation during Gods wrath of Jesus and for his word, which had not worshipped the beast or his image, neither taken the mark, was resurrected to live and reign with Christ for a thousand years Rev 20:4. The rest of the dead remained so until after a thousand years Rev. 20:5, where they stood judgement before the great white throne. They were then judged by the laws of the books and their own works actions, and if their name was not found in the book of life they were cast into the lake of fire to be eternally tormented Rev. 20:11-15.

At which time after the thousand years Satan is let loose for a short season to deceive the nations of the earth and gather them together at Gog and Magog, to surround the city of the saints and make war: and God will devour them with fire from heaven Rev. 20:7-9. And Satan will then be cast into the lake of fire with the Beast and False Prophet, to be tormented for ever and ever Rev. 20:10.

NEW HEAVEN AND NEW EARTH

After the passing of the seals, Gods Wrath, the great war of Gog and Magog and the white throne judgement; comes a new heaven and a new earth, filled only with land and no sea Rev. 21:1. And brought down from heaven was the holy city, New Jerusalem, and living within the city and among men was Yeshua Rev. 21:2-3. And there was no more tears, no more death, no more sorrow, and no more pain Rev. 21:4. The city will be surrounded by a great and high wall, with twelve gates, three on each side and guarded by a angel at each; each gate had the name of one of the twelve tribes of Israel written on it, and the wall had twelve foundations with the Apostles names written upon them. The cities Height, length and width were equal measuring at 1500 miles Rev. 21:11-16. The wall is measured at 216 feet high, and the wall is of *jasper*, and the city as clear as pure gold, like transparent glass Rev. 21:18. The foundations were each garnished with different stones; Jasper, sapphire, chalcedony, emerald, sardonyx, sardius, chrysolite, beryl, topaz, chrysoprasus, jacinth and amethyst, and the twelve gates each are of pearls Rev. 21:19-21.

Within the city lies no temple as Yahweh is the temple. The city has no need for light of the sun, moon or stars, as the light of Yeshua shines through it. The gates will never be shut and there shall never be night Rev. 21:22-27. Flowing from the throne of God, is a river of pure and crystal clear water with trees of life on both sides, with twelve different manners of fruit growing from them which yields every month, and the leaves are the healing of the nations. The saints will finally see the face of God and will have his name written upon their foreheads Rev. 22:1-4.

What a beautiful picture of the new heaven and new earth is given. It is going to be such an awesome sight to see and a glorious feeling to live, within and amongst our Lord and Savior.[xviii] [xix]

ARE YOU READY?

ACKNOWLEDGEMENTS

Pastor Tim Foster for content verification.

Brother in Christ, Nathan Cotten, for being a sounding board and confidant regarding material and content in preparation for this narrative.

Chaplain Doug Hogsten for Biblical counsel on the subject matter.

Sister Pricilla Foster for initial proofreading and editing.

Sister Ana Alvarez for creating the books cover image.

Brother in Christ, Robert Mendez, for financial contributions toward publishing.

If you are interested in having R. S. Henzerling teach a class or conference on Revelation and the End Time Prophecy, please feel free to contact him through his e-mail at rshenzerling@gmail.com.

APPENDIX

The King James Version of the Holy Bible is the primary source for all references in this book.

---

i Sun Tzu "The Art of War"

ii http://www.bible.ca/rapture-origin-john-nelson-darby-1830ad.htm

iii Here is a little "historical soup" for the mix. As you will see—the predominate position of the 1st through 4th centuries knew nothing of the common pre-trib position which is embraced today. They held something like most—but not all—early Pentecostal leaders did.

1. Barnabas ca 40-100 "The final stumbling-block or source of danger approaches, concerning which it is written…for the whole past time of your faith will profit you nothing, unless now in this wicked time we also withstand the coming sources of danger, as becometh the sons of God. That the Black One may find no means of entrance…Epistle of Barnabas 4.
2. Justin Martyr 100-168 "…He shall come from heaven with glory, when the man of apostasy, who speaks strange things against the Most High, shall venture to do unlawful deeds on the earth against us the Christians…" Dialogue with Trypho, 110.
3. Melito 100-170 "…For with all his strength did the adversary assail us, even then giving a foretaste of his activity among us

[during the Great Tribulation] which is to be without restraint." Discourse on the Resurrection 1,8

4. Irenaeus of Lyons 140-220 "It is manifest, therefore, that of these [potentates], he who is to come shall slay three, and subject the remainder to his power, and that he shall be himself the eighth among them. And they shall lay Babylon waste, and burn her with fire, and shall give their kingdom to the beast, and put the Church to flight. After that they shall be destroyed by the coming of our Lord." Against Heresies Book 5 26.228.
5. Tertullian 150-220 "…the souls of the martyrs" are taught to wait for beneath the altar, whilst they earnestly pray to be avenged and judged: taught, I say, to wait… that the beast Antichrist with his false prophet may wage war on the Church of God…" On the Resurrection of the Flesh, 25
6. Hipploytus 160-240 "…the one thousand two hundred and three score days during which the tyrant is to reign and persecute the Church…" Treatise on Christ and Antichrist, 61.
7. Cyprian 200-258 "…the day of affliction has begun to hang over our heads, and the end of the world and the time of Antichrist to draw near, so that we must all stand prepared for the battle…" Epistle 55, 1
8. Lactantius 240-330 "…and power will be given him to desolate the whole earth forty-two months…righteousness will be cast out, and innocence hated…then the righteous followers of truth shall separate themselves from the wicked, and flee into solitudes…" Divine Institutes VII, 17
9. Jerome 340-420 "…I told you that Christ would not come unless Antichrist had come before…" Epistle 21.
10. Chrysostom 345-407 "…because that [the time of Antichrist] will be a sign of the coming of Christ…" Homilies on First Thessalonians 9
11. Augustine 354-430 "…but he who reads this passage, even half asleep, cannot fail to see that the kingdom of Antichrist shall

fiercely, though for a short time, assail the Church…" The City of God XX, 23

iv http://christinprophecy.org/articles/the-origin-of-the-concept-of-a-pre-tribulation-rapture/

v Jeffrey Brickle & Jeremy Painter 2017, Handbook on the General Epistles and Revelation, WAP Academic a division of word aflame press

vi Blaising, Craig A.; Bock, Darrell L.November 1993. Progressive Dispensationalism. Wheaton, IL: Bridgepoint Books

vii Robin Johnston, PhD General Editor; Lee Ann Alexander, MA, Managing Editor; Apostolic Study Bible ; Hazelwood, MO; Word Aflame Press

viii https://davidjeremiah.blog/seven-churches-of-revelation-bible-study/

ix https://bible.org/seriespage/7-message-sardis-rev-31-6

x https://davidjeremiah.blog/4-steps-to-reviving-your-faith-from-johns-letter-to-the-church-of-sardis/

xi Douglas Connelly 2007, The Book of Revelation Made Clear, Zondervan Books

xii http://biblestudycourses.org/revelation-bible-study-courses/revelation-4-1-11-exploring-the-passage/

xiii Jeffrey Brickle & Jeremy Painter 2017, Handbook on the General Epistles and Revelation, WAP Academic a division of word aflame press

xiv Jeff Kinley 2015, Wake the Bride, Harvest House Publishers

xv Jeffrey Brickle & Jeremy Painter 2017, Handbook on the General Epistles and Revelation, WAP Academic a division of word aflame press

xvi Jeffrey Brickle & Jeremy Painter 2017, Handbook on the General Epistles and Revelation, WAP Academic a division of word aflame press

xvii biblehub.com, pulpit commentary

xviii http://www.signs-of-end-times.com/

xix Thomas Nelson Bible, Thomas Nelson a division of HarperCollins Christian Publishing, inc.

ABOUT THE AUTHOR

R. S. Henzerling is a faithful member of the Temple Christian Center in Temple, Texas. He proudly serves beside his wife on the church's leadership team and other church ministries. He is ordained as a minister by the Apostolic World Christian Fellowship and has been fascinated with prophecy since he was a boy. He spent twenty years in the military, including four combat tours, and holds numerous degrees. He is launching a church ministry to help veterans and their families.